FOLLOWING
THE LEADERSHIP AND LOVE OF
JESUS

Dr. Bruce W. Smoll

FOLLOWING THE LEADERSHIP AND LOVE OF JESUS
By Dr. Bruce W. Smoll

ISBN: 979-8-9878735-5-7

All Rights Reserved. No part of this publication may be produced or transmitted in any form or by any means without written permission of the author. The author guarantees all contents are original and do not infringe upon the legal rights of any other person or work.

Prepared for Publication By

B|B
PUBLISHING

MAKING YOUR BOOK A REALITY
Cedar Point, NC | 843-929-8768 | info@BandBpublishingLLC.com

Scripture quotations marked KJV are taken from The Holy Bible, King James Version.

Scripture quotations marked NKJV are taken from the New King James Version®. Copyright © 1982 by Thomas Nelson. Used by permission. All rights reserved.

Scripture quotations Marked NIV are taken from THE HOLY BIBLE, NEW INTERNATIONAL VERSION®, NIV® Copyright © 1973, 1978, 1984, 2011 by Biblica, Inc.® Used by permission. All rights reserved worldwide.

Scripture quotations marked NLT are taken from the Holy Bible, New Living Translation, copyright © 1996, 2004, 2015 by Tyndale House Foundation. Used by permission of Tyndale House Publishers, Inc., Carol Stream, Illinois 60188. All rights reserved.

Scripture quotations marked PHILLIPS are taken from The New Testament in Modern English by J.B Phillips copyright © 1960, 1972 J. B. Phillips. Administered by The Archbishops' Council of the Church of England. Used by Permission.

To contact the author: hvlm1955@gmail.com
His Victorious Life Ministry

CONTENTS

ENDORSEMENTS 1
INTRODUCTION 3
CHAPTER 1 5
Integrity
CHAPTER 2 9
Honesty
CHAPTER 3 13
Dedication
CHAPTER 4 17
Optimism
CHAPTER 5 25
Humility
CHAPTER 6 31
Gentleness
CHAPTER 7 37
Companionship
CHAPTER 8 43
7 Lessons from the Life of Jesus
CHAPTER 9 53
The Confirmation of His Leadership
CHAPTER 10 67
The Confirmation of Our leadership
CHAPTER 11 79
Am I A Leader?
CHAPTER 12 87
Am I Willing To Follow Jesus As My Leadership Role Model?
CHAPTER 13 97
How Do I Lead Like Jesus?

Endorsements

Dr. Bruce Smoll brings a lifetime of experience to the subject of Leadership. He has held leadership positions in the military, in business and in the Church. This experience coupled with his love for Jesus has led Dr. Bruce on this journey of "Following the Leadership and Love of Jesus". No matter where you are in your leadership journey or in your relationship with Jesus, the principles in this book will help you become a better leader and disciple of Jesus.

Dr. Doug Sands –
Academic Dean, Restoration College International
Fairmont, WV
Senior and Founding Pastor, OASIS Worship Center
Stonewood, WV

Dr. Bruce Smoll has made a wonderful contribution

to the copious teachings on Leadership available to the Body of Christ. In his new book, Following The Leadership and Love of Jesus, he points out the vital character qualities ensuring that a leader will not only be successful in their endeavors, but will be around for the "long haul." Many individuals who have "leadership gifts" and appear to be successful may not be there in the future if their leadership style is not "character based." Bruce points out the necessity for both "gifts and character" as we see modeled in the Life of Jesus Christ who is our primary example of a leader. The book also helps the reader to examine themselves as a leader, and also the steps to take in becoming a leader like Jesus Christ. The writer uses examples of success and failure from his own experience as a leader in the US Army. I suggest that all those pursuing a leadership role at home, work or in church read this important book and learn to lead effectively.

Dr. John Polis
Revival Fellowship International, Inc.

Introduction

There have been many leaders that have risen to power throughout history, some practiced barbaric war tactics in conquering their enemies while others manipulated people with their compelling words. Although these tactics seemed effective in the short run, the leaders were eventually overthrown because of their selfish views on how to lead others.

Out of all the leaders in the world, there is only one that has made a lasting impact for the better, and that is none other than Jesus the Messiah. He had many qualities that are essential to effective leadership and over the course of this book I would like to present to you what I believe are seven of His key leadership points, and then in the second half of this writing we will look more at how we can follow the leadership and love of Jesus.

Dr. Bruce W. Smoll

Chapter 1

INTEGRITY

Integrity is the act of behaving honorably, even when no one is watching. People with integrity follow moral and ethical principles in all aspects of life.

As children, we told lies whenever we thought we could use them to get our way. Then through the wise counsel we may receive from parents, grandparents, pastors, etc., we begin to mature, seeing that telling the truth even when it does not benefit us will always produce the best results in the long run. I was hard-headed about this, so it took me longer than some people to follow the path of integrity.

This Key Leadership Point should extend from our personal life, all the way through to professional areas at work such as decision-making, interacting with colleagues, and serving customers or clients.

Additionally, employers who are committed to hiring those with integrity will be better equipped to provide high-quality service and maintain a positive reputation. When employees have integrity, their managers can trust their team is working diligently.

Let us take a look at this first key leadership point in the life of Jesus when He was tempted by the devil in Matthew 4.

TEMPTATION 1
Doubt the Word of God

> *Then was Jesus led up of the Spirit into the wilderness to be tempted of the devil. 2 And when he had fasted forty days and forty nights, he was afterward an hungred. 3 And when the tempter came to him, he said, If thou be the Son of God, command that these stones be made bread. 4 But he answered and said, It is written, Man shall not live by bread alone, but by every word*

that proceedeth out of the mouth of God. Matthew 4:1-4 KJV

TEMPTATION 2
Twist the Word of God

Then the devil taketh him up into the holy city, and setteth him on a pinnacle of the temple, 6 And saith unto him, If thou be the Son of God, cast thyself down: for it is written, He shall give his angels charge concerning thee: and in their hands they shall bear thee up, lest at any time thou dash thy foot against a stone. 7 Jesus said unto him, It is written again, Thou shalt not tempt the Lord thy God. Matthew 4:5-7 KJV

TEMPTATION 3
Reject the Word of God

Again, the devil taketh him up into an exceeding high mountain, and sheweth him all the kingdoms of the world, and the glory of them; 9 And saith unto him, All these things will I give thee if thou wilt fall down and worship me. 10 Then saith Jesus unto him, Get thee hence, Satan:

for it is written, Thou shalt worship the Lord thy God, and him only shalt thou serve. Matthew 4:8-10 KJV

The devil tried to bribe Jesus with all the riches of the world, but even when He was vulnerable and no one else was around, Jesus refused to give in, and through integrity, He had victory over Satan.

The devil aimed to make Jesus a fake Messiah, abusing the Divine gifts for selfish ends. Jesus, who came 'to destroy the works of the devil,' first triumphed over Satan in His conflict by honoring the Word of God even when no one was watching. Jesus was a man of Integrity.

Chapter 2

HONESTY

What is honesty? Many children think honesty means you "don't tell a lie", and speaking the truth is a big part of being honest. But honesty means more than "not lying." Honesty means your actions are truthful also. If you must hide what you are doing because you are trying to deceive someone, you are not being honest. In simple words, honesty is about both speaking and acting truthfully.

Jesus was truly a man of honesty. He never lied nor cheated anyone in His lifetime. He emphasized the importance of honesty when he said, in Matthew 5

But let your communication be, Yea, yea; Nay, nay: for whatsoever is more than these cometh of evil. Matthew 5:37 KJV

The two great evils into which we are liable to fall into when our communication is more than yea and nay, are dishonesty and disrespect.

Relationships are built on trust and dishonesty destroys that trust. When two people trust each other, they feel safe and secure, but trust does not happen overnight. It takes the consistency of engaging in honest communication and unselfish acts over a long period of time for people to truly trust someone else. However, even after a lifetime of consistency, trust can be shattered by just one act of dishonesty. After that foundation of trust is destroyed it can be very difficult to rebuild.

Have you ever been deceived or lied about by someone you thought was a good friend? If so, then you know the feelings of hurt and betrayal that resulted from that dishonesty. There is little doubt that dishonesty can destroy the fabric of precious relationships.

Now, let us take a look at disrespect? The definition

of disrespect is to insult someone or display rude behavior by showing a "lack of respect." It can come in many forms but centers around the idea that another person's feelings have been impolitely disregarded.

Relationships are built on trust, honesty, and appreciation for the other person. Healthy, respectful relationships leave both parties feeling validated and heard. In a disrespectful relationship, one can feel angry, hurt, and abused because they do not feel valued due to trust, honesty, and boundaries being intentionally broken.

If the abusive and disrespectful behavior is not halted, it can lead to tension, which in turn can cause increased conflict, and in the end, it could lead the relationship to fall apart whether that be in a friendship, marriage, or even employment.

Let us remember that the two virtues of truthfulness and reverence are closely connected and are the foundation of all those who follow Christ.

> *... Everyone that is of the truth heareth my voice. John 18:37b KJV*

Christ came into the world to bear witness of the truth. Any Christian profession which does not spring from the love of truth and the fear of God is unworthy of the name it bears. Therefore, in reflecting either on our physical life or our innermost feelings and convictions these are the two principles to which we must adhere, and which we must pray to God for confirmation and strengthening of our hearts. Jesus was a man of Honesty.

Chapter 3

DEDICATION

What is dedication? Dedication is the act of being fully devoted to something, whether this is something intangible, such as a task, goal, or desired outcome, or something that you are physically a part of, such as a cause, religion, sports teams, or another person. What does dedication look like? Simply put, you can tell that someone is dedicated to something when the glamour of any job, person, or cause is gone, but their internal devotion keeps them going even when what you are dedicated to, at the moment seems to be no longer fun or exciting.

At one point or another, anything worth anything

in life will be challenging and it is only our dedication, our full devotion to that person, cause, or job that will aid us in being successful.

Now to our main subject at hand, the leadership of Jesus. He was dedicated and fully devoted to doing the will of His Father God in Heaven. We see throughout the Old Testament that God wanted His people in full health, so that is what Jesus did. We read in Acts 10,

> *How God anointed Jesus of Nazareth with the Holy Ghost and with power: who went about doing good, and healing all that were oppressed of the devil; for God was with him. Acts 10:38 KJV*

We see a picture of this in Matthew's Gospel,

> *"And Jesus put forth his hand, and touched him, saying, I will; be thou clean. And immediately his leprosy was cleansed." Matthew 8:3 KJV*

> *"Then saith he to the man, 'Stretch forth thine hand.' And he stretched it forth; and it was restored whole, like as the other." Matthew 12:13 KJV*

You would think that everyone would love what Jesus did, healing people and bringing deliverance to their lives, but they did not. The religious leaders seemed to always question Him when He was doing what His Father wanted Him to do. Here is the point, Jesus could have been a little less devoted to God and been a little more accepted by men, but His dedication to God outweighed His desire for acceptance of men.

Jesus also knew that His mission was to save the lost even though He was again being questioned and rejected by the religious leaders.

> *And it came to pass, that, as Jesus sat at meat in his house, many publicans and sinners sat also together with Jesus and his disciples: for there were many, and they followed him. 16 And when the scribes and Pharisees saw him eat with publicans and sinners, they said unto his disciples, How is it that he eateth and drinketh with publicans and sinners? Mark 2:15-16 KJV*

The greatest example of Jesus' dedication, His full devotion to His Father, was accepting God's plan of redemption for mankind, even when that plan included dying a horrific death on the cross. Jesus was a man of dedication.

Chapter 4

OPTIMISM

Optimism is a mental attitude characterized by hope and confidence in a successful and positive future. A person who is an optimist expects good things to happen, they see the brighter side of life. This perspective on life will produce an attitude that is linked to several benefits, including better-coping skills, lower stress levels, better physical health, and higher persistence when pursuing goals.

From the perspective of an optimist, hardships, and difficulties are not viewed as the end of the world but as learning experiences or temporary setbacks. Even the most miserable day holds the promise for them that "tomorrow will probably be better."

Shortly before I retired from the United States Army. I worked with a senior NCO that told me I needed to change my thought process. He told me that I was a half-glass-full kind of person. I did not understand what he was telling me at first. But after several weeks of sitting and talking with him, I began to understand and knew I had to make some changes in my life. I had to turn negative thinking into positive thinking. The process is simple, but it does take time and practice, I had to create a new habit.

Jesus was an extremely optimistic leader. He faced the challenges of life knowing that God would never leave Him. When Jesus was resurrected, He told His disciples,

> *"Peace I leave with you, my peace I give unto you: not as the world giveth, give I unto you. Let not your heart be troubled, neither let it be afraid." John 14:27 KJV*

These are life-changing words, but not just on this earth alone. They touch a force above the world. These words, in their Divine consciousness of vast spiritual power, in their distance from the strife and trouble of men, they are of that true supernatural which abides in the secret of God.

What was this peace? It was not peace from the absence of outward pains that strike life. The Jewish and the Roman world, the Church and State, were all against the disciples of Christ. Because of this the disciples were driven into deserts, thrown to the beasts, stoned, and butchered to make a Roman holiday.

Was it freedom from the unrest of the heart, freedom from sorrow and care, or the bitter pain of thought and love? No, because even Jesus faced pain, He suffered as we suffer.

So how do we define this peace? It is a spiritual peace in the deep region of the human spirit, peace in that inner life, striking its thoughts into eternity, and it is linked unbrokenly to God. In that deep Life in Christ, there is entire and perfect peace.

It is:

1. Peace that comes through the fulfillment of duty.

2. Peace that comes from the Triumph of Love. It

is in the depth of God's love that His peace was rooted.

3. Christ's peace consisted of conscious union with God. "I and My Father are One." And because Christ had it, and was one of us, we will not give up hope no matter how ugly and dim the battle we fight gets." Peace, I leave with you, My peace I give to you."

This inward peace is what Paul calls peace with God. This phrase refers to the pacification of conscience. Faith accepts God's gift of His Son as a sincere gift; it seeks to be reconciled, to be justified, and forgiven. Through Christ, the sinful man finds that He has recovered that peace with God, which is the absence of all condemnation.

In this spiritual submission to God, Jesus, in His spiritual character, is our great example. To it, His great atonement for our sins is our great compeller to model our lives after Him. To this loving subjection, let us strive continually to bring ourselves, so that we may have peace and confidence in Him. There are many sorrows and disturbances to contend with in this life on earth, yet giving up and relegating the hope of inward peace will not do. We do not have to wait until our time on earth is done to have this peace because Christ had it here while on this earth. More childlike confidence in the Father and Son, more profound submission to our Father's will; and surely the Spirit, who is the Dove, will descend, and breathe sweet repose wherever His white wings brood. Surely, He will make His nest within your spirit; and then, while storms surge and beat around your every step in this life, you shall have the peace of Christ throughout the ages.

Peace With All

Let us take the word "peace" in at least some of the senses which our Savior would give to it.

Peace within ourselves. We may be extremely prosperous, and yet there is a secret pang that makes us ill at ease. Or there is something of which we do not like to speak, of which we do not like to hear, and if possible, we would rather not think. But in Christ, we can be at peace within ourselves knowing that our righteousness is not dependent on our perfection, but upon His.

Peace with one another. Christ, Himself was the great Peacemaker. In Him, Jew, Gentile, Greek, and

Barbarian came together and were one. This is not talking about one in our pursuits of career and interests, not one in our tastes and preferences, and not one in our opinions, but one in belief and submission to Christ. Therefore, we should never let the differences between us, become a cause of separation. Just to bring clarification, the only cause of separation that should occur in the body of Christ between believers is known sin in the life of a Christian. While the door for repentance should always be held wide open, as we see in 1 Corinthians 5, when Paul was referring to the man in known sin with his mother-in-law, we should separate ourselves from any follower of Christ who is openly and knowingly practicing sin with no intention of repentance. But if we see the evidence of repentance, to ensure peace with one another in the Body of Christ, welcome them back.

There are occasions when truth and justice must be preferred to peace, whether in nations, churches, or private life, but this use of justice should always be to bring peace in whatever the circumstance may be. This is why we see war in our world as sometimes inevitable. But these are the exceptions, and we must be very careful not to multiply the exceptions lest we should make them the rule of life.

The peace of the Holy Spirit of Christ is something much wider and deeper than outward diversities or likenesses. "Not as the world giveth," not as to outward appearance giveth, not as the mere letter giveth, but as the Spirit, speaking to our inmost spirits, so is the peace which Christ gives to His disciples.

Peace with God. Think of God, the one Eternal Judge, perfectly just and perfectly merciful, who sees not as man sees, who knows whereof we are made, who knows our ignorance and our blindness, who sees us exactly as we are, and not as the unjust, erratic world sees us. That thought is the peace of God the Father. We can certainly live life confidently knowing that Jesus holds our future. He was a man of optimism.

Dr. Bruce W. Smoll

Chapter 5

HUMILITY

Humility is perhaps one of the more underrated qualities in our world. It is highly praised when seen in the life of a person, but rarely taught as a character trait to be attained and sought after. You could almost say that humility is looked at as old-fashioned in our selfie society, where even when people are helping others, they seem to let the whole world know what they are doing. This is not what Jesus taught.

> *"Take heed that you do not do your charitable deeds before men, to be seen by them. Otherwise, you have no reward from your Father in heaven. 2 Therefore, when*

you do a charitable deed, do not sound a trumpet before you as the hypocrites do in the synagogues and the streets, that they may have glory from men. Assuredly, I say to you, they have their reward. 3 But when you do a charitable deed, do not let your left hand know what your right hand is doing, 4 that your charitable deed may be in secret; and your Father who sees in secret will Himself reward you openly. Matthew 6:1-4 NKJV

Just because humility is looked at as old-fashioned does not mean that it is no longer important. Humility is a vital part of developing proper self-esteem, self-worth, and confidence because humility could be properly defined as having the correct estimation of who you are and who you are not. This does not mean you have low self-esteem, but you understand you are not more important than others, while at the same time, you are not less important than others. You know how to succeed and how to let others succeed.

In other words, humility is not being a 'doormat' and allowing people to walk all over you. Instead, it is an understanding that every human is equally valuable, a recognition that you are worth no more or less than anyone else.

One of the reasons why humility seems old-fashioned is that we are often made to feel that we need to look out for ourselves because nobody else will do so. "It's a dog-eat-dog world, you know!" This point of view suggests that you need to be aggressive to get what you need in life, which, along with pride, is perhaps the very opposite of humility.

For many of us, humility is one of the hardest traits to develop, because it must start from a recognition that you are not always right and that you do not have all the answers. It also requires an acceptance of yourself of where you are at this moment in your life, which many of us find challenging.

Stay Humble

It is easy to be humble when you are at the bottom of the ladder, as it were: new in a job. The more you progress, however, the more likely you are to have people looking to you for answers, and the more you find yourself believing that you can help. When you find yourself in this position, if you are not careful, you can reach higher rungs in the ladder and forget where you came from. The truth is, the higher you go, the more important humility seems to become, Jesus illustrated this truth with this parable,

> *So He told a parable to those who were invited when He noted how they chose the best places, saying to them: 8 "When you are invited by anyone to a wedding feast, do not sit down in the best place, lest one more honorable than you be invited by him; 9 and he who invited you and him come and say to you, 'Give place to this man,' and then you begin with shame to take the lowest place. 10 But when you are invited, go and sit down in the lowest place, so that when he who invited you comes he may say to you, 'Friend, go up higher.' Then you will have glory in the presence of those who sit at the table with you. 11 For whoever exalts himself will be humbled, and he who humbles himself will be exalted." Luke 14:7-11 NKJV*

Servant Leadership

One of Jesus' trademark attributes was servant leadership. He demonstrated humility by washing the feet of His disciples,

> *"After that, He poured water into a basin and began to wash the disciples' feet, and to wipe them with the towel with which He was girded." John 13:5 NKJV*

Just a few days before Jesus obtained the Name above all names, becoming the King of kings, and the Lord of lords, when He completed living a sinless life and was fully obedient to God by dying on the cross for our sins He was washing the disciple's feet. Right before He got to the "top of the ladder" He was still humbly serving others. Jesus did not boast of being clothed in fine linen nor did He have a grand palace to live in. However, He set the precedent of humility as the key to getting people to respect you as a leader.

> *"Let this mind be in you, which was also in Christ Jesus, 6 who, being in the form of God, did not consider it robbery to be equal with God, 7 but made Himself of no reputation, taking the form of a bondservant, and coming in the likeness of men. 8 And being found in appearance as a man, He humbled Himself and became obedient to the point of death, even the death of the cross. 9 Therefore God also has highly exalted Him and given Him the*

name which is above every name, 10 that at the name of Jesus every knee should bow, of those in heaven, and of those on earth, and of those under the earth, 11 and that every tongue should confess that Jesus Christ is Lord, to the glory of God the Father." Philippians 2:5-11 NKJV

Jesus was a man of humility.

Chapter 6

GENTLENESS

Gentleness consists of kindness, consideration, and likability. However, gentleness is not being a "pushover" where you allow others to control you when the situation is unjust or unfair. Gentleness is when justified and properly focused righteous anger is applied to produce godly results. Gentleness is a strong hand with a soft touch. It is a tender, compassionate approach toward others' weaknesses and limitations. A gentle person still speaks the truth, sometimes even the painful truth, but in doing so they guard their tone so the truth can be well received.

Gentleness is the virtue of doing good with the

least possible harm to others. This is one area I needed a lot of help. God led me to a team called "KAIROS" (a prison ministry). This is where I learned gentleness. The prisoners do not need harsh words, they need someone to talk with them from a stance of God's love, or benevolence. Gentleness is courage without violence, strength without harshness, and love without anger. Gentleness gains its strength from its steady and stable foundation. Gentleness is a constant strength born from serenity and patience that contrasts with the turmoil of outrage, wrath, vengeance, and violence. It is amazing, I learned gentleness from the incarcerated.

The quality of gentleness takes our focus off of our wants and desires and puts the focus on building bridges with others; "When you focus on want, you become an endless cycle of wants. To get, simply release, and then gently invite." WHOSE QUOTE IS THIS?

As a leader, Jesus promoted peacefulness and gentleness in how He led his disciples. He did not practice a dictatorship style of leadership but communicated God's heart in a way that made people's hearts turn towards Him. He strongly valued peace, so much that he stated in, Matthew 5

"Blessed are the peacemakers: for they shall

be called the children of God." Matthew 5:9 KJV

Peacemakers are not the people who simply want peace or long for peace. They are not the governments that pass laws on peace, or legislators who write policies on peacekeeping. Peacemakers are those whom the Lord God uses to bring reconciliation, or restored relationship to a fallen world. As Christians, we have peace with God through faith and have been made ministers of reconciliation, so those fallen sinners may be reconciled back to God and gain true peace in their hearts.

> *"Therefore if any man be in Christ, he is a new creature: old things are passed away; behold, all things are become new. 18 And all things are of God, who hath reconciled us to himself by Jesus Christ, and hath given to us the ministry of reconciliation; 19 To wit, that God was in Christ, reconciling the world unto himself, not imputing their trespasses unto them; and hath committed unto us the word of reconciliation. 20 Now then we are ambassadors for Christ, as though God did beseech you by us: we pray you in Christ's stead, be ye reconciled*

to God. 21 For he hath made him to be sin for us, who knew no sin; that we might be made the righteousness of God in him." 2 Corinthians 5:17-21 KJV

God in His grace has reconciled those who believe in the Lord Jesus to Himself, and through Christ, we have been given this important ministry of reconciliation, so that the world may know that God is the Lord and Savior of mankind. Christ came to earth to reveal God's goodness and grace, and His death on the cross opened the way for fallen man to find peace with God, and to be reconciled back to Him through faith in His Son.

During Christ's absence from the earth, those who believe in His name have been entrusted with a lifework that proclaims the gospel of grace to a lost world, so that men, who are dead in their sin and estranged from God, may know the truth, be saved by grace through faith in Christ and find peace with God. Jesus came so that the world might be reconciled back to their Father, and we are called to be His peacemakers.

Man seeks empty happiness and longs for peace in a world at war, but the child of God who has been saved by grace through the sacrificial work of Christ on Calvary's cross gains more than happiness. He is blessed to be reconciled to God and to have peace with Him through the forgiveness of sin. But there is so much more, we have been promised when we rest in Him and walk in spirit and truth, His peace will guard our hearts and guide our path.

Our initial salvation brings peace with God but during our walk of faith through the journey of life, we can enjoy the peace of God. God's continuous, divine peace in our hearts. Jesus told His confused disciples just before He was to walk to the cross,

> *"Let not your heart be troubled, you believe in God, believe also in Me." John 14:1 KJV*

We who believe can receive that peace that passes understanding as we remain in the right relationship with the Father, through faith in the Son. But we are also given the authority to go into the world as God's peacemakers. We are to be witnesses to the truth of the gospel and preach the truth to every creature, that peace with God is possible by His grace, through faith in Christ. Jesus was a man of peace and gentleness.

Dr. Bruce W. Smoll

Chapter 7

COMPANIONSHIP

Companionship, "A feeling of friendship or fellowship." A person's tendency to seek companionship and establish new social connections is constant throughout one's life.

We see from the life of Jesus that He chose His companions, His disciples, carefully. I believe each one of the twelve that He spent the majority of His time with was chosen by the leading of the Holy Spirit. I also believe that Jesus is the ideal model of the companion that I want to become. During His earthly ministry whether dealing with literal storms or spiritual storms,

He never left His disciples and always looked for ways to add value to them.

Below are just a few insights and tips on companionship.

Spending time with others

Spending time with others, whether doing elaborate activities or just sitting and talking, is a straightforward way to begin building companionship. Gradually increasing the depth of conversation is a natural progression for people who already spend a lot of time together and can help develop the feelings of friendship and fellowship that define companionship. However, some people may simply have no desire to expand their social circles, or they do not feel companionship for you, just as you may not feel companionship for everyone you spend time with. Companionship develops naturally and should not be forced.

Sharing your honest emotions

Sharing honest emotions is essential in a romantic relationship to keep trust with your partner and to better understand one another. Companionship in a romantic relationship means that each partner has an emotional need to confide in the other and keeping the lines of communication open is necessary to maintain the intimacy between you. Without that kind of openness, it is easy for partners to lose the feeling of companionship and for the relationship to become boring or end entirely.

Staying interested in them.

Taking the same level of interest in your partner as you did when you started dating and were eager to know more is a wonderful way to keep your conversations fresh and exciting. You can also try a new hobby or activity that the other enjoys. Share the stories that have not yet been told such as childhood memories, funny things that happened at work, plans, and other personal feelings to continue nurturing the companionship between the two of you.

Expanding our thought of companionship outside of a dating or marriage relationship, the connection can happen on several levels or any combination of those levels. Some people have compatibility because of their connection or interest in musical or literary arts, while others might be intrigued by politics or economics. Many people simply enjoy learning, while critiquing and debating newly processed information.

Companionship is about being good company for the person we have chosen to share our life with. My wife and I have good companionship and are best friends. We do not just love each other; we genuinely like each other too. And we enjoy spending time together. We make time to be with each other, and we share common values and common views about what is good and bad. We have common goals in life and are willing to support each other to make those goals a reality. As a team, keeping God, Jesus, and The Holy Spirit at the center of all we do is the most important part of our companionship.

Compatibility is encouraged by the willingness to both teach and learn from one another. You may not especially enjoy modern art but might find pleasure in visiting new exhibits with your partner, who is enthusiastic about it. Conversely, you might look forward to taking them to a film festival. It is an opportunity to share something meaningful to you with someone you love. When either or both parties in a relationship are rigid in terms of what they consider stimulating, the relationship will be less rewarding.

The importance of connection

Having friends, acquaintances, co-workers, and

other companions with whom to socialize can help develop a feeling of togetherness so you do not feel alone in everyday life. Feelings of loneliness can manifest as a vague and constant sense of worry. Over time, these feelings can be detrimental to your immune system because they act on the fight-or-flight instinct, resulting in stress when there is no enemy to confront or from which to escape.

Companionship during the teenage years

During the teenage years, friendships are important for several reasons. Teens typically spend more time with their peers than they do with their parents, siblings, or other social contacts. Therefore, friends influence many aspects of their life. Healthy friendships can help them avoid delinquency, isolation, and many of the negative characteristics that are associated with this period of life.

Healthy friendships help teenagers feel accepted and confident and can pave the way for the development of other positive social ties. Confidence and feeling accepted are integral characteristics of their social and emotional development. When a teenager feels as if he or she is part of a group, they are less likely to be negatively affected by bullying and other forms of rejection. Teens who feel confident and accepted may also be less likely to engage in the bullying of others.

Friends can be a positive influence in the academic, social, and personal aspects of a teenager's life. Because they often share common goals and/or interests, they can persuade a teen to make good choices and help prevent irresponsibility and conflict, encourage success, and provide the basis for a larger network that will be helpful later in life. Friendships can also help a teen get back on track with his/her goals and/or plans when other, more negative influences are present.

The teenage years are often very stressful. Having trustworthy, loyal friends is important to help them deal with the stress and uncertainty that is a normal part of development. That is why is it so important for parents and godly adult influences in a teen's life, to help guide them to choose healthy and godly circles of friends.

Back to the life of Jesus, with those He chose to spend the most time with, He never left them and always looked for ways to add value to them. Jesus was a man of companionship.

Chapter 8

7 LESSONS FROM THE LIFE OF JESUS

So far, we have covered seven points of leadership in the life of Jesus; integrity, honesty, dedication, optimism, humility, gentleness, and companionship. While there are many more that could be listed, I believe these were key leadership points in His life. Now, I would like to look at seven lessons we can learn from Jesus being asleep in the boat while in the middle of the storm found in Matthew's Gospel.

> *"And when he was entered into a ship, his disciples followed him. 24 And, behold,*

there arose a great tempest in the sea, insomuch that the ship was covered with the waves: but he was asleep. 25 And his disciples came to him, and awoke him, saying, Lord, save us: we perish. 26 And he saith unto them, Why are ye fearful, O ye of little faith? Then he arose and rebuked the winds and the sea, and there was a great calm. 27 But the men marveled, saying, What manner of man is this, that even the winds and the sea obey him!" Matthew 8:23-27 KJV

Why is Jesus asleep in the storm? Just a few verses before, the Bible says,

When the evening was come, they brought unto him many that were possessed with devils: and he cast out the spirits with his word, and healed all that were sick: Matthew 8:16 KJV

The compassion and care Jesus had for the multitude of people was evident in all the miracles He had performed. It was then time for Jesus and His disciples to cross over to the other side of the lake away from the crowds of people, and that is what Jesus commanded His disciples to do. What these disciples were not expecting was the very sudden change in the weather, when a dangerous and fierce storm came upon the lake.

One can only imagine how tired Jesus must have been after ministering to and healing the crowds because the Bible says He was asleep in the middle of what the disciples considered to be a life-threatening situation. But even something that seemed so life-threatening to them was no match for Jesus' power and authority. After Jesus calmed the storm, the disciples were utterly amazed and in awe that the winds and the waves obeyed Him.

This amazing account in the Bible inspires us to have deeper faith and trust in God. Here are seven important lessons we can learn from this story.

LESSON 1
Follow Jesus Regardless

Following Jesus, it sounds easy enough, but following Him is not always our natural inclination, or always going to result in the easy path in life. But following Him will produce God's best in our life.

Think about it, each of the disciples chose to follow

Him into the boat, but then life got harder, even life-threatening. However, unless they followed Him, they would have never seen the amazing power He operated in on their behalf when He calmed the storm. Every day will have its challenges and every day we have the choice whether or not to follow Jesus – to be like Him, to bear the fruit of the Spirit, and to make decisions in line with God's word and the purpose He has for each of us.

Jesus invites us to follow Him and be like Him,

> *"Then spake Jesus again unto them, saying, I am the light of the world: he that followeth me shall not walk in darkness, but shall have the light of life." John 8:12 KJV*

As a follower of Jesus, we will see His power and goodness in us and through us.

LESSON 2
Battles In Life Are Certain

The storm that rolled upon the lake was sudden, and even with Jesus right there in the boat, the disciples still thought they would lose their lives. From this story, we learn that the hardships and unexpected battles in life are certain. Every follower of Jesus is going to encounter troubles in this life.

> *"These things I have spoken unto you, that in me ye might have peace. In the world ye shall have tribulation: but be of good cheer; I have overcome the world." John 16:33 KJV*

We will endure opposition, and hardship, and make mistakes. Sometimes, we are tempted to think that when we are going through tough situations, God must be punishing us.

What this story reveals is that the storm was not Jesus' way of punishing the disciples. The troubles of life will come because we live in a fallen, broken world until Jesus' return. This story teaches us that challenges are unavoidable, but we can put our hope in the Lord just as the disciples did when they finally called out to Him.

LESSON 3
God Is With You

Even though we are guaranteed to face less-than-desirable or painful situations in life, this story teaches us that God is with us. Jesus did not get off the boat and abandon His disciples; He was with them the entire time.

We sometimes feel alone when things get tough. We wonder if God has left us on our own to fend and fight for ourselves. Scripture reminds us repeatedly that God is always with us. He does not leave us nor forsake us.

> *And the Lord, he it is that doth go before thee; he will be with thee, he will not fail thee, neither forsake thee: fear not, neither be dismayed. Deuteronomy 31:8 KJV*

We can put our trust in Him because God is faithful and does not break His promises.

> *That by two immutable things, in which it was impossible for God to lie, we might have a strong consolation, who have fled for refuge to lay hold upon the hope set before us: Hebrews 6:18 KJV*

He is with us always.

LESSON 4
Call Out To Jesus

This story invites us as followers of Jesus to call out

to Him. We do not know how long the storm raged, but it was long enough for the disciples to believe they were going to perish in the storm. They finally did the right thing and called out to Jesus for help.

When you are going through circumstances that seem hopeless or are at a loss for how to move forward, call out to Jesus. God hears every prayer, and His ear is open to those who call upon His name.

> *"But verily God hath heard me; he hath attended to the voice of my prayer." Psalm 66:19 KJV*

We can bring every need to the Lord who cares for us, loves us, and has good plans for those who love Him. We can call out to Him in praise, in surrender, and when we are struggling. This account teaches us to call out to Jesus in our need.

LESSON 5
It Is Good To Rest

Jesus went to sleep when He got on the boat. He was tired from healing, casting out spirits, and being with so many people. So, He rested. Jesus was good at resting and finding moments to get away and find time with the Father.

God wants each of us to rest, as well. God gave us the Sabbath, and Jesus even reminded His followers to come to Him for real rest and renewal.

> *"Come unto me, all ye that labour and are heavy laden, and I will give you rest."*
> *Matthew 11:28 KJV*

Jesus modeled the perfect life for us. We get tempted to believe that staying busy and driven is what makes us good, however, rest is important. When we look at Jesus in this story, we learn that rest and taking care of ourselves is good and something that God desires for us as His beloved children. It is good to slow down and find moments to rest in God's presence.

LESSON 6
God Has Authority Over Everything

As the disciples reflected in awe, even the winds and waves obeyed Jesus. God has authority over everything. We may not always understand exactly what that means or how God uses His power in each situation, but we can rest confidently knowing that God is in control over our lives and this world.

> *"I am the Lord, and there is none else, there*

> *is no God beside me: I girded thee, though thou hast not known me: 6 That they may know from the rising of the sun, and from the west, that there is none beside me. I am the Lord, and there is none else. 7 I form the light, and create darkness: I make peace, and create evil: I the Lord do all these things." Isaiah 45:5-7 KJV*

We are not at the mercy of the evil one, rather, we have God on our side and fighting our battles. In this story, we learn that God has authority over everything, and we do not have to live in fear.

> *"For I the Lord thy God will hold thy right hand, saying unto thee, Fear not; I will help thee." Isaiah 41:13 KJV*

LESSON 7
You Do Not Have To Be Afraid

When the disciples woke Jesus, He questioned the fear in their life and their lack of faith. They were afraid and thought they were going to die even when Jesus was with them. What this story shows us is that we do not have to live in fear, even in the scariest or tumultuous circumstances.

We have all been in the disciples' shoes and have experienced fear. What this passage demonstrates is that we do not have to be afraid of the fearful storms we face in life if we put our faith in God. It takes faith to put our trust in Him rather than be fearful, especially when we are facing difficult or painful situations. We can trust God through it all and know He is on our side.

> *"Yea, though I walk through the valley of the shadow of death, I will fear no evil: for thou art with me; thy rod and thy staff they comfort me." Psalm 23:4 KJV*

The account of Jesus sleeping on the boat while the storm was raging is one that provides many valuable teachings. It shows us the reality of life and the goodness of God toward us in every situation. I am in awe that Jesus can calm even the most ferocious of storms. We do not have to be afraid when life is uncertain; we can have faith in Jesus. When we follow Jesus, He will be there for us, and we can completely trust in Him.

Chapter 9

THE CONFIRMATION OF HIS LEADERSHIP

Let us say you are giving a talk to a group of children. You are dressed in a robe like a character from Bible times and tell them, "I have something to tell you, something I have never told anyone else before." You open the robe to reveal a big S on your T-shirt. "Kids, I am Superman!"

The children would laugh and challenge you. "If you're Superman, fly up to the ceiling!"

Then you must explain to them, that many people

make claims about who they are, but not everyone can offer proof. The problem is that once you tell them that you are Superman, you must prove it.

> *"You are still challenged. Being challenged is a place of growth and that is a good place to be." (John Maxwell)*

Leadership works that way. Whenever anyone says, "*I'm a leader,*" that person will be put to the test. He or she must back that claim with proof. What kind of proof? Well, the most obvious kind of proof that a person is a leader is that he or she has followers. If you do not have followers, you are not a leader.

Followers are people who believe in you and trust you enough to follow you. They endorse your leadership by saying to you, "*I recognize your leadership ability. I trust you. I want to be like you. I want to learn from you. I want to go where you lead me.*"

A leader is, by definition, a person who works through and with other people to achieve a goal or a vision. A president sets a vision or direction for the nation, then commissions his staff and his cabinet to achieve that vision, works with Congress to enact that vision, and encourages the people to embrace that vision. A corporate CEO casts a vision for the company, works through the management team to implement that vision, and motivates the workforce to fulfill that vision at every level. A pastor articulates a biblically based vision for the church and works through the church board, the elders and deacons, the teachers and youth workers and volunteers, and all the members to transform that vision into a Christ-centered ministry.

The ultimate role model of effective leadership is Jesus Christ. During His earthly ministry, Jesus worked through and with people to achieve the vision called "The Kingdom of Heaven." He began by calling to Himself a circle of twelve people from assorted and diverse backgrounds, including fishermen (Simon, Andrew, James, and John), antigovernment political extremists (Simon the Zealot and Judas Iscariot), and a pro-government collaborator (Matthew the tax collector). Jesus mentored these followers, taught them, challenged them, and united them into a unified force focused on a single goal. Then He pushed them out of their comfort zones and delegated important tasks to them and founded His church through them.

Jesus worked through the Twelve to establish a church that has endured for two thousand years and now circles the globe. He inspired trust and followership in the people He met. As they followed and watched His life, they became witnesses, confirming that He truly was the Messiah, the leader promised in the Old Testament, anointed by God, descended from David, and sent to save His people.

Jesus also shared His vision with a wider circle of disciples and with the crowds, and He inspired confidence and enthusiasm about His vision of a coming kingdom. In the process of casting His kingdom vision and teaching in parables, He enabled people to see His vision for themselves, and He drew many people to His vision. Jesus the Messiah created a community of people who were focused on His kingdom vision, and by leading, teaching, motivating, and inspiring those people, He changed the world.

As we see in John's gospel, Jesus offered seven basic proofs, seven distinct confirmations that He was truly the Messiah, God's anointed leader. After we examine those seven proofs, we will see how to apply the lessons of the leadership style of Jesus to every leadership arena— governments and corporations, churches and schools, military units and sports teams, and the most intimate leadership arena of all, the home.

PROOF 1
The Witness Of God The Father

The first proof Jesus offers to confirm His leadership role is the witness of God the Father. He told His hearers,

> *"And the Father himself, which hath sent me, hath borne witness of me..." John 5:37a KJV*

What did Jesus mean? He was speaking about the Father's stamp of approval and confirmation that God issued publicly after Jesus was baptized by John the Baptist. In Matthew's gospel, we read:

> *"And Jesus, when he was baptized, went up straightway out of the water: and, lo, the heavens were opened unto him, and he saw the Spirit of God descending like a dove, and lighting upon him: 17 And lo a voice from heaven, saying, This is my beloved Son, in whom I am well pleased." Matthew 3:16-17 KJV*

In the presence of John, the Baptist, and many other witnesses, God the Father openly announced His eternal relationship between Himself and Jesus of

Nazareth. Here we see a stark contrast between Jesus and every other so-called "messiah" who claims to come in the name of God. For example, Joseph Smith, the founder of Mormonism, claimed he was all alone at night on a wooded hill when he was visited by an angel; that angel, he said, revealed a new religion to him out of a book of golden plates. Muhammad, the founder of Islam, entered Jerusalem by night and claimed to hear the voice of God speak to him while he was alone.

Go through the history of various religions and you hear repeated claims of *"in the middle of the night, when no one else was around, God spoke to me."* But Jesus did not have to make unverified claims of a revelation by night. God the Father openly confirmed His Son as the anointed Messiah.

On a less public occasion, Jesus took His three closest disciples, His executive committee as it were, to a mountain (later known as the Mount of Transfiguration). What these three disciples witnessed that night is recorded in Mark's gospel:

> *"And after six days Jesus taketh with him Peter, and James, and John, and leadeth them up into an high mountain apart by themselves: and he was transfigured before*

them. 3 And his raiment became shining, exceeding white as snow; so as no fuller on earth can white them. 4 And there appeared unto them Elias with Moses: and they were talking with Jesus. 5 And Peter answered and said to Jesus, Master, it is good for us to be here: and let us make three tabernacles; one for thee, and one for Moses, and one for Elias. 6 For he wist not what to say; for they were sore afraid. 7 And there was a cloud that overshadowed them: and a voice came out of the cloud, saying, This is my beloved Son: hear him. 8 And suddenly, when they had looked round about, they saw no man any more, save Jesus only with themselves." Mark 9:2-8 KJV

The messiahship of Jesus was confirmed as He conversed with Elijah and Moses, and as the voice of God said, "This is my beloved Son." Jesus was not a self-proclaimed, self-anointed leader. His right to be called Jesus the Messiah was proclaimed by God the Father, and that proclamation was heard by many witnesses.

PROOF 2
The Witness Of John The Baptist

The opening chapter of John's gospel reveals the testimony of a second witness, John the Baptist:

> *"And John bare record, saying, I saw the Spirit descending from heaven like a dove, and it abode upon him. 33 And I knew him not: but he that sent me to baptize with water, the same said unto me, Upon whom thou shalt see the Spirit descending, and remaining on him, the same is he which baptizeth with the Holy Ghost. 34 And I saw, and bare record that this is the Son of God." John 1:32-34 KJV*

As Jesus later said of John the Baptist,

> *"Ye sent unto John, and he bare witness unto the truth." John 5:33 KJV*

John the Baptist, who called himself *"the voice of one crying out in the wilderness,"* in John 1:23 was a forerunner and a witness for Jesus, a man sent by God with a unique ministry to confirm to the world the identity of Jesus the Messiah.

PROOF 3
The Witness Of Jesus Himself

It may seem strange that Jesus called Himself to the witness stand to testify to His ministry as God's anointed Messiah. But after referring to the confirming witness of His Father and John the Baptist, Jesus said,

> *But I have greater witness than that of John: for the works which the Father hath given me to finish, the same works that I do, bear witness of me, that the Father hath sent me. John 5:36 KJV*

Later, Jesus said, "I and the Father are one" (John 10:30). His hearers understood exactly what He was saying, and they picked up stones to stone Him to death. They justified their intention to kill Him in the following verse.

> *The Jews answered him, saying, 'for a good work we stone thee not; but for blasphemy; and because that thou, being a man, makest thyself God.' John 10:33 KJV*

On another occasion in John 14:7, Jesus told the people that because they had seen Him, they had seen God the Father.

Jesus did not merely claim to have a unique and eternal relationship with God. Everything about His life backed up this claim.

Through the evidence of His life, Jesus made it clear that He was a leader to be followed.

PROOF 4
The Witness Of The Holy Spirit

As we have already noted, the Holy Spirit gave His blessing and confirmation at the baptism of Jesus by descending on Him like a dove and remaining on Him. Even though the story is presented to us beautifully, in symbolic language, there are undoubtedly depths to the witness of the Spirit in the life of Jesus that we do not fully comprehend. But we do know that the Holy Spirit confirmed the ministry and leadership of the Lord Jesus. The presence of the Spirit gave Jesus the authority to preach the gospel and perform a variety of miracles.

PROOF 5
The Witness Of Scripture

The Old Testament confirmed the leadership of Jesus. Prophets foretold His coming, His messianic ministry, and His death. Some of the most explicit prophecies about Jesus were written by the prophet Isaiah. He pictured the birth of Jesus (Isaiah 9:6), the suffering of Jesus (Isaiah 53:4-10), the servanthood of Jesus (Isaiah 42:1-4), and even the announcement of Jesus by John the Baptist (Isaiah 40:3). Many other messianic passages, such as Psalms 22, 69, 110, and 118, speak vividly of Jesus's life, ministry, Lordship, rejection by Israel, death, and resurrection.

As the Lord Jesus told the corrupt religious leaders who persecuted Him,

> *Search the scriptures; for in them ye think ye have eternal life: and they are they which testify of me. 40 And ye will not come to me, that ye might have life. John 5:39-40 KJV*

PROOF 6
The Witness Of Miracles

The ministry of Jesus was confirmed by the miracles He performed. John's gospel refers to them as "signs." Though John mentions fewer miracles than any of the other gospel writers, the signs He mentions bear witness to the purpose, power, and leadership authority of Jesus.

It is important to understand that Jesus did not perform these signs as an act of showmanship. An attention-seeking actor would have performed magic tricks to amaze and attract the crowds. Jesus often performed His most amazing miracles quietly, out of public view, and He frequently told witnesses to tell no one. His reluctance to perform miracles to play to the crowd confirms His words,

> *"I do not accept glory from human beings."*
> *John 5:41 NLT*

PROOF 7
The Witness Of The Disciples

The disciples traveled with Jesus throughout His earthly ministry. They saw what He did, heard His teachings, and believed. When the religious leaders persecuted Jesus and He spoke openly of the hardship of following Him, many would-be disciples turned away. Only a few continued to follow.

Those who continued with Christ included Simon Peter, who said, *"Lord, to whom shall we go? Thou hast the words of eternal life." John 6:68 KJV*. In saying that, Peter did not merely mean that Jesus knew the rules of life or could explain how life should be lived; he meant that Jesus himself was the Source and Giver of eternal life.

The author of the gospel of John was himself a follower of Jesus. In the next to last verse of his gospel, John says,

> *"This is the disciple which testifieth of these things and wrote these things: and we know that his testimony is true." John 21:24 KJV*

Dr. Bruce W. Smoll

Chapter 10

THE CONFIRMATION OF OUR LEADERSHIP

We who participate in leadership today can hardly claim to possess the unique qualifications of Jesus the Messiah. But by observing His life, we learn this important leadership principle: The call to leadership must be confirmed.

What if someone walked into your office and said, *"I have come to lead you into truth"*? First, such an approach would be so strange that you would call security to have that person removed.

But suppose something about this person's manner made you want to examine his claims. How would you know who he was? How would you evaluate the authority of his claim? How would you know if this person could lead you to the truth or not? You would ask a few practical questions: *"By what right or authority do you speak? What are your qualifications or credentials? Could I see your résumé? Do you have any references?"*

A person cannot simply come out of nowhere and expect to be followed as a leader. A leader must prove himself or herself skilled to lead. This is true whether one is a leader in the religious realm or the secular realm.

A pastor of a church must overcome several hurdles to achieve a position of leadership. Normally, a pastor is first trained and then ordained (formally recognized as someone called by God as a spiritual leader). Anyone can train for leadership, but only God calls people to spiritual leadership. It is also good for upcoming Pastors to serve as an apprentice under another senior pastor, this allows them to grow into leadership, and to become mentally, emotionally, and spiritually more mature. Throughout this process, church leaders and members have an opportunity to observe and recognize the upcoming pastor's unique gifts and abilities.

Authentic spiritual leaders are also confirmed by people outside the church. The apostle Paul, when giving instructions to his disciple, Timothy, about ordination, said that an authentic spiritual leader,

> "...must also have a good reputation with outsiders, so that he will not fall into disgrace and into the devil's trap." 1 Timothy 3:7 NIV

This rule of confirmation applies in secular leadership settings as well. Whether in business, government, the military, academia, or even the home, people must earn the right to lead. I may believe that I have been divinely appointed to head Apple Computer, but if I walked into Apple headquarters in Cupertino, California, and announced,

"I'm here to take over," I assure you they would not usher me into the CEO's office. Most likely, I would be ushered to the parking lot.

If I would like to become the CEO of a major corporation, I will have to go through a process of confirmation. I will have to start at the bottom and be patient. I will have to listen, learn, be mentored, and instructed, demonstrate initiative and creativity, acquire skills, make friends and influential connections, and gradually move up the corporate ladder. At each level of my career, some individual or more likely, a group of individuals will have to examine my work, assess my character, and say, *"Yes, he is ready. He has earned a chance to move up to the next level."*

Many would-be leaders lack the patience to climb that ladder. Full of excessive pride and the arrogance of youth, they do not even know how much they do not know. So, they insist that they have what it takes to lead.

I learned over my twenty years in the U.S. Army, how to separate in the interview stage the leadership contenders from the pretenders. The most obvious sign of a pretender is a candidate who tells you that your organization is desperate for someone with his ability, and he will save your organization. That kind of arrogance is always a red light.

I have also seen, in both the Christian and secular worlds, people who looked great on paper, who had impressive résumés, but who proved incapable of leading once they were hired and placed in the hot seat.

They did not have the skill to lead, and they lacked the approval of other people.

Leadership is tough, but you must grow in God, walk in your calling, and reach your destiny. God does not demand perfection, but He wants our diligence. This means a willingness to work hard even when things are tough, the ministry is small, or we face rejection for taking an unpopular stand.

Diligence is what sets leaders apart from dreamers. Anyone can set goals and hope to carry out wonderful things, but few will work persistently toward them, refusing to quit even when it gets hard.

Jesus is the perfect leader. He did not back down, no matter how hard it got—even to the point of death. He made people angry because He spoke the truth, and He knew that death awaited Him on the cross, yet "He steadfastly set His face to go to Jerusalem," (Luke 9:51-53) where His death would take place.

We may not die for Christ as a martyr, but we will all experience many little deaths as we follow God and lead others.

There is death to our pride, to our freedom, and to our "right" to do whatever we want when we want.

Jesus said those seeking to be great must be the *"servant of all" (Mark 9:35).*

Leadership starts by serving Jesus in worship and prayer, drawing close to Him, and then serving His people. The more we become like Him, the more we will serve as He does.

Some people have a wrong picture of leadership, thinking that it is about control or having power over people, but Jesus addresses this also:

> *But Jesus called them to Himself and said to them, "You know that those who are considered rulers over the Gentiles lord it over them, and their great one's exercise authority over them. 43 Yet it shall not be so among you; but whoever desires to become great among you shall be your servant." Mark 10:42-43 NKJV*

Christ's way is different from the world, yet for all who walk in it, there is a blessing of supernatural strength—divine aid that helps us stay true to the task.

Leaders are not always the most skilled or educated people—the disciples certainly were not! Leaders simply must be faithful, teachable, and obedient. There is also a willingness to act, take responsibility, and take risks.

Currently, God is calling forth bold men and women who refuse to play it safe by avoiding conflict and trying to please everyone. Leaders must act, pursue righteousness, and call others into a radical and holy lifestyle.

True leaders have a sense of purpose. They move themselves and others toward it. This focus dictates their actions. And when they make mistakes, they dust them off quickly and return to the path.

The Lord honors those who faithfully do what He commands. The story in Matthew 25 of the servants who received large sums of money (called talents) is a prime example:

> *"For the kingdom of heaven is like a man traveling to a far country, who called his servants and delivered his goods to them. 15 And to one he gave five talents, to another two, and to another one, to each according to his own ability; and immediately he went on a journey. 16 Then he who had received the five talents went and traded with them, and*

made another five talents. 17 And likewise he who had received two gained two more also. 18 But he who had received one went and dug in the ground, and hid his lord's money. 19 After a long time the lord of those servants came and settled accounts with them. 20 "So he who had received five talents came and brought five other talents, saying, 'Lord, you delivered to me five talents; look, I have gained five more talents besides them.' 21 His lord said to him, 'Well done, good and faithful servant; you were faithful over a few things, I will make you ruler over many things. Enter into the joy of your lord.' 22 He also who had received two talents came and said, 'Lord, you delivered to me two talents; look, I have gained two more talents besides them.' 23 His lord said to him, 'Well done, good and faithful servant; you have been faithful over a few things, I will make you ruler over many things. Enter into the joy of your lord.' 24 "Then he who had received the one talent came and said, 'Lord, I knew you to be a hard man, reaping where you have not sown, and gathering where you have not scattered seed. 25 And I was afraid, and went and hid your talent in the ground. Look, there you have what is yours." Matthew 25:14-25 NKJV

A man (or master, who symbolizes God) gives his servants different amounts of money to invest while he is away on a journey. Two of the servants work hard and double the money they received. The man rewards both servants the same, honoring their diligence more than the specific amount of money they had.

But the third servant, who received the least amount of money, hid it in the ground because he was afraid of losing it. On the day of reckoning, he gave his master the same amount that he had been given. Because he refused to take risks, he had no increase. This displeased the master, greatly:

> *But his lord answered and said to him, 'You wicked and lazy servant, you knew that I reap where I have not sown, and gather where I have not scattered seed. 27 So you ought to have deposited my money with the bankers, and at my coming I would have received back my own with interest. 28 So take the talent from him, and give it to him who has ten talents. 29 'For to everyone who has, more will be given, and*

he will have abundance; but from him who does not have, even what he has will be taken away. 30 And cast the unprofitable servant into the outer darkness. There will be weeping and gnashing of teeth.'"
Matthew 25:26-30 NKJV

Spiritualizing our rationale for not stepping into leadership is not an excuse before the Lord. Whatever resources the Lord has given us we are required to use. The stakes are high, but He will honor with His strength every effort we make to obey.

Leading others is necessary for God's kingdom—to reach the lost and see the Gospel reach the ends of the earth.

Set your heart to pursue the journey of leadership, walking in reliance on Christ, who has overcome the world (John 16:33). Much trial, joy, and reward await!

Before He ascended to Heaven, Jesus gave His followers a basic command for what to do next. These words have served as "marching orders" for generations of Christians:

"Go therefore and make disciples of all the nations, baptizing them in the name of

> *the Father and of the Son and of the Holy Spirit, 20 teaching them to observe all things that I have commanded you; and lo, I am with you always, even to the end of the age." Amen. Matthew 28:19-20 NKJV*

Many of us have taken these simple instructions, known as the Great Commission, and overcomplicated them. We have made sharing our faith a terrifying and fearful task. But it does not have to be.

To grow in our leadership, we must be faithful to where we are.

Dr. Bruce W. Smoll

Chapter 11

AM I A LEADER?

There is a way to lead that honors God and restores health and effectiveness to organizations and relationships. It is the way Jesus calls us to follow as leaders: to serve rather than be served.

Anytime you seek to influence the thinking, behavior, or development of people toward carrying out a goal in their personal or professional lives, you are taking on the role of a leader.

As you begin your journey of leading like Jesus, you must answer the following three key questions, which we will now explore over these last three chapters.

1. Am I a leader?

2. Am I willing to follow Jesus as my leadership role model?

3. How do I lead like Jesus?

1. Am I a Leader?

Leadership is a process of influence. It can be as intimate as words of guidance and encouragement to a loved one or as formal as instructions passed through extended lines of communication in organizations. Leadership can be nurturing the character and self-worth in children and promote greater intimacy and fulfillment in personal relationships, or it can involve distributing diverse resources in an organization to accomplish a specific objective and or task.

Each of the following situations describes someone engaged in an act of leadership:

- A mother with a child any time of day.

- A friend who risks alienation to confront a moral failure.

- A corporate executive who rejects offers of inside information to gain a competitive edge.

- A U.S. Navy SEAL commander who orders his troops into harm's way to succeed in their mission.

- Spouses who seek mutual agreement on day-to-day finances.

- A middle school teacher who excites curiosity in the minds of her students.

- A rehabilitation nurse who patiently oversees the anger of a stroke victim.

- A missionary doctor who refuses to leave his patients, even in the light of being captured by enemy forces.

- An adult who provides advice and guidance on living arrangements to his aging parent.

- A terminally ill patient who demonstrates grace, confidence, courage, and calmness to anxious loved ones.

- A local government official who takes an unpopular political stand based on their principles.

- A dictator who hoards millions.

- A local pastor who avoids teaching on controversial issues for fear of rejection.

- A high school coach who does not confront rule violations by his star player.

Two things are clear in this list. First, each of these people is a leader because he or she is affecting or influencing others, either positively or negatively. This list reveals that some leadership actions are specific (a dictator hoarding millions), and others are more general (a mother with a child); some are clear (an official taking an unpopular stand), and some are done in secret (a pastor avoiding teaching on a controversial issue). The actions of a leader that create influence are not always obvious to those being led. We also influence people who may not choose to follow, such as the executive who refused insider information.

Second, these leaders participate in making a personal choice about how and to what end they will use their influence. It is the same choice we are all called to make when we exert influence on people: do we seek to serve or to be served? If your driving motivations are self-promotion and self-protection, you will use your influence with others to fulfill your needs. If your actions are driven by service and dedication to a cause or a relationship, then you will model and encourage these values in others.

As you think about the many ways you influence the actions of other people, you can see that you are a leader wherever you go, not just at work. Whether you serve others as a parent, spouse, family member, friend, or citizen, or whether you have a leadership title and position like CEO, Pastor, coach, teacher, or manager—you are a leader!

As we consider how we can lead like Jesus in our various leadership roles, we need to be aware of the difference between life role leadership and organizational leadership.

Life Role Leadership functions in enduring relationships (parent, spouse, sibling, friend, and citizen) and focuses on growing and developing people and supporting mutual commitment in the relationship. It involves seasons of personal sacrifice to promote spiritual and physical well-being. It is based on duty, honor, and lifelong obligation and is resilient based on the level of relational commitment and anticipates love, loyalty, trust, mercy, patience, forgiveness, and sacrifice. It also values love, compassion, trust, commitment, honesty, and grace.

Organizational Leadership involves positions and titles, bestowed at the convenience of the organization, to serve the perceived needs and culture of the organization.

Measured accountability for long and short-term results under constant scrutiny by a variety of stakeholders (investors, governing boards, employees, customers, analysts, alumni, unions, regulatory agencies, partners, congregations, and constituencies).

At-risk based on performance and preferences of governing bodies and stakeholders, power and influence are prone to conflict agendas and priorities (finance versus marketing, engineering versus manufacturing, church staff versus lay leadership, staff versus operations).

Sensitive to shifts in organizational structure, standards, and priorities (mergers and acquisitions, reorganizations, outsourcing, and alliances), rewards are delivered in the form of additional power, material rewards, and recognition.

Operate in the realm of competition and marketplace standards and biases (globalization, technology, demographics, trends, and fashion),

Values competence, material results, vision, courage, diligence, confidence, conviction, and integrity.

The most dramatic difference between life role leadership and organizational leadership involves the stability of the relationships the leader is trying to influence.

Take a moment to pause and reflect on or about the people who have most influenced your thinking, behavior, and life path. As you recall their names and faces, you will realize that leadership, titles, and positions of organizational authority are only part of the leadership landscape. Now think of all the relationships in which you can influence the thinking and behavior of others, and consider how often in any given situation you face the choice: *"Am I seeking to serve or to be served?"* The answer to that question will depend on whom we choose to follow.

Dr. Bruce W. Smoll

Chapter 12

AM I WILLING TO FOLLOW JESUS AS MY LEADERSHIP ROLE MODEL?

We have looked at the first question, Am I A Leader? Now, let us look at the second key question, Am I Willing to Follow Jesus, as my leadership role model?

You might say, *"Before I look to Jesus as my leadership role model, I need to understand what leading as Jesus means."* The spirit and the core concept of leading like Jesus are summarized in the *"not be so among you"* mandate that Jesus gave to His disciples about how they were to reach and conduct roles of leadership. In Matthew 20, we read,

> *But Jesus called them to Himself and said, "You know that the rulers of the Gentiles lord it over them, and those who are great exercise authority over them. 26 Yet it shall **not be so among you**; but whoever desires to become great among you, let him be your servant. 27 And whoever desires to be first among you, let him be your slave— 28 just as the Son of Man did not come to be served, but to serve, and to give His life a ransom for many." Matthew 20:25-28 NKJV (emphasis added)*

This call by Jesus to servant leadership is clear and unmistakable; His words leave no room for plan B. He placed no restrictions or limitations on time, place, or situations that would allow us to exempt ourselves from His command. For followers of Jesus, servant leadership is not an option; it is a mandate. Servant leadership is to be a living statement of who we are in Christ, how we treat one another, and how we demonstrate the love of Christ to the entire world. If this sounds like serious business with intense responsibilities, it is!

The exciting part of leading like Jesus is that He never sends us into any situation alone or with a flawed plan or a plan to fail. Jeremiah 29 tells us,

> *For I know the thoughts that I think toward you, says the Lord, thoughts of peace and not of evil, to give you a future and a hope. 12 Then you will call upon Me and go and pray to Me, and I will listen to you. 13 And you will seek Me and find Me, when you search for Me with all your heart. 14 I will be found by you, says the Lord... Jeremiah 29:11-14 NKJV*

As in all things, when Jesus speaks to us about leadership, He speaks about what is right and effective. We can trust His Word as an expression of His unconditional love and sacrifice for our eternal well-being. As followers of Jesus, we can trust Him regardless of our circumstances, and we can freely ask Him to give us wisdom in all things, including our leadership roles. James 1 reminds us that Jesus wants to be intimately involved in all aspects of our lives:

> *When all kinds of trials and temptations crowd into your lives my brothers, don't resent them as intruders, but welcome*

them as friends! Realise that they come to test your faith and to produce in you the quality of endurance. But let the process go on until that endurance is fully developed, and you will find you have become men of mature character with the right sort of independence. And if, in the process, any of you does not know how to meet any particular problem he has only to ask God—who gives generously to all men without making them feel foolish or guilty—and he may be quite sure that the necessary wisdom will be given him. But he must ask in sincere faith without secret doubts as to whether he really wants God's help or not. The man who trusts God, but with inward reservations, is like a wave of the sea, carried forward by the wind one moment and driven back the next. That sort of man cannot hope to receive anything from God, and the life of a man of divided loyalty will reveal instability at every turn. James 1:2-8 PHILLIPS

A common barrier to embracing Jesus as a leadership role model lies in skepticism about the relevance of His teaching to your specific leadership situations. We are, in many ways, faced with the same questions that Peter faced when Jesus asked him to do some highly unusual and unorthodox things regarding his fishing business.

Here was the situation as described in Luke 5:

> *One day as Jesus was preaching on the shore of the Sea of Galilee, great crowds pressed in on him to listen to the word of God. 2 He noticed two empty boats at the water's edge, for the fishermen had left them and were washing their nets. 3 Stepping into one of the boats, Jesus asked Simon, its owner, to push it out into the water. So he sat in the boat and taught the crowds from there. 4 When he had finished speaking, he said to Simon, "Now go out where it is deeper, and let down your nets to catch some fish." 5 "Master," Simon replied, "we worked hard all last night and didn't catch a thing. But if you say so, I will let the nets down again." 6 And this time their nets were so full of fish they began to tear! 7 A shout for help brought their partners in the other boat, and soon both boats were filled with fish and on the verge of sinking. 8 When Simon Peter realized what had happened, he fell to his knees before Jesus*

and said, "Oh, Lord, please leave me—I'm such a sinful man." 9 For he was awestruck by the number of fish they had caught, as were the others with him. 10 His partners, James and John, the sons of Zebedee, were also amazed. Jesus replied to Simon, "Do not be afraid! From now on you will be fishing for people!" 11 And as soon as they landed, they left everything and followed Jesus. Luke 5:1-11 NLT

What do you think was going through Peter's mind when he replied, *"Master, we have been fishing all night and we haven't caught a thing?"* It sounds like he might have been thinking something like this: *"I have been listening to Jesus address the crowds with great power and wisdom. I respect Him as a teacher and for His knowledge of God's Word. But now He has asked me to do something that goes totally against my knowledge and instincts about how to run my business. He does not know about fishing. I know fishing and fishing are my business, and this is not a practical plan. If I do what He says, it is going to be a waste of time and energy, and my workers are going to wonder if I have lost my mind."*

Peter's skepticism, however, did not prevent him from taking a leap of faith because of who gave him the instructions. Because of his faith, he experienced miraculous results, and he was stunned by what he believed was too great a gap between himself and what Jesus would need from him.

Jesus sought to calm Peter's doubts and fears and invited to be transformed for a higher purpose. And He is issuing the same call to us. Jesus knows fish. He also knows your business, whether it is in the service of an organization or a life role.

One way of putting Jesus to the test would be to apply the same criteria to His knowledge, experience, and success that you would to the hiring of a business consultant. Take a few minutes and consider if you would hire Jesus as your leadership consultant in your life role leadership or organizational leadership positions based on His earthly experience.

> *Because He Himself suffered when He was tempted, He is able to help those who are being tempted Hebrews 2:18 NIV*

> *For we do not have a high priest who is unable to empathize with our weaknesses, but we have one who has been tempted in every way, just as we are—yet he did not*

sin. 16 Let us then approach God's throne of grace with confidence, so that we may receive mercy and find grace to help us in our time of need. Hebrews 4:15-16 NIV

In addition to His leadership resume, Jesus understood from years of personal experience the challenges of daily life and work. Although Jesus was God, He was not ashamed to do a man's work. He spent the first thirty years of His life on earth as a worker, a carpenter of Nazareth. We can never sufficiently realize the wonder of the fact that Jesus understands a day's work and knows the difficulty of making ends meet. He knows the frustration of ill-mannered customers and clients who will not pay their bills. He knows the difficulties of living in an ordinary home and in a big family, and He knows the problems that bother us in this everyday world.

Think about how Jesus would do your job differently than you would. As the following scriptures suggest, Jesus wants to do His work in you and through you:

Come to me, all you who are weary and burdened, and I will give you rest. 29 Take my yoke upon you and learn from me, for I am gentle and humble in heart, and you will find rest for your souls. Matthew 11:28-29 NIV

I am the vine; you are the branches. If you remain in me and I in you, you will bear much fruit; apart from me you can do nothing. John 15:5 NIV

If you remain in me and my words remain in you, ask whatever you wish, and it will be done for you. John 15:7 NIV

"If you love me, keep my commands. 16 And I will ask the Father, and he will give you another advocate to help you and be with you forever— 17 the Spirit of truth. The world cannot accept him because it neither sees him nor knows him. But you know him, for he lives with you and will be in you. 18 I will not leave you as orphans; I will come to you. John 14:15-18 NIV

If you are skeptical about adopting Jesus as your leadership role model, write down your reasons. What is it about Jesus that is causing you to doubt? What is it about you that is causing you to hold back?

Dr. Bruce W. Smoll

Chapter 13

HOW DO I LEAD LIKE JESUS?

Even if you have concluded that you are a leader and that you are willing to follow Jesus as your leadership role model, because He has the leadership resume to respond to the issues you face, you may be asking, *"How do I lead like Jesus?"*

Learning to lead like Jesus is more than an announcement; it is a commitment to lead differently. This change will not happen overnight. In fact, we believe leading like Jesus is a life-changing cycle that begins with personal leadership and then moves to leading others in one-on-one relationships, then to leading a team or group, and finally, to leading an organization or community. We feel this sequence is true in both life role leadership and organizational leadership roles.

During His time on earth, Jesus poured His life into the training of His disciples in the first three leadership areas: personal leadership, one-on-one leadership, and team leadership. During that process, He equipped them to follow His leadership mandate after He was gone as they moved to the fourth level: organizational leadership.

Personal Leadership

Personal Leadership is effective leadership that starts on the inside. Before you can hope to lead anyone else, you must know yourself. This is called personal leadership because it involves choice.

Every leader must answer two critical questions:

1. Whose am I?

2. Who am I?

The first question, *"Whose am I?"* deals with choosing the primary authority and audience for your life. In other words, whom are you trying to please? Leaders often demonstrate whose they are by how they define success in today's world. They think success has to do with earthly power and position, as well as performance and the opinions of others.

You can state it any way you like, but Scripture teaches us that, we are created to please God. In the personal leadership arena, you first must choose whether you will please God.

The second question— *"Who am I?"*—deals with your life purpose. Why did the Lord put you on earth? What does He want to do through you? Scripture teaches that true success is the fulfillment of the life mission God planned for you. Your success in life depends on your relationship with Christ and what level of control you will let Him have in your life. Are you willing to surrender all to Him and to live as He would have you live, rather than how you want to live?

The natural outcome of deciding to please God as well as turning over control of your life to Him is a change in your perspective. If you live a life that is not designed to please God or give Him control, your perspective will be inward and focused on yourself. If you live your life to please God and put him in charge, your perspective will be outward and characterized by God-given confidence that will lead your life.

Jesus had to answer these questions.

Early in His ministry, Jesus demonstrated His desire to please only the Father and to turn control of His life over to Him. Jesus made His choice public when He surrendered all to His Father and insisted that John baptize Him "to fulfill all righteousness" (Matthew 3:15).

Jesus's desire to please the Father was demonstrated even more dramatically after His baptism when He went into the wilderness and was tempted by Satan (Matthew 4:1-11). The events recorded for us in the Gospels show us that during this time Jesus had to decide whose He was and who He was. Would He live by the mission His Father had given Him for the accomplishment of His Father's purpose or Satan's purpose? In all these situations, Jesus chose the will of His Father.

Paul had to answer these questions.

A fitting example of life-changing personal

leadership is the apostle, Paul. He was born in Tarsus, a pure Hebrew of the tribe of Benjamin (Philippians 3:5). He was educated as a rabbi and lawyer in Jerusalem under Gamaliel, one of the greatest teachers of the Law of the day (Acts 22:3). So, he knew God's Word. He passionately persecuted Christians and pursued them as they fled Jerusalem, even to Damascus, which was 130 miles away.

Then he met Jesus on the road to Damascus (Acts 9:5). During his dramatic encounter with Jesus, Paul was blinded by a light and remained blind for three days until Ananias laid hands on him as the Lord had commanded. Through the power of the Holy Spirit, Paul's sight was restored. He was baptized and then began to declare boldly in the synagogues that Jesus was the Son of God. As a result, his life was threatened (Acts 9:20–25).

He went alone into Arabia and after a time returned to Damascus (Galatians 1:15–19). After three years of preaching, Paul finally arrived in Jerusalem, where he met the other disciples, and his ministry to the Gentiles was confirmed.

The apostle Paul had the knowledge he needed. He had gone through a lengthy period of preparation.

He knew the Word of God. When he finally met Jesus, he made a heart commitment. However, that did not mean he was ready to minister. His first enthusiasm did not generate the results he hoped for. So, he went to Arabia and spent time with God, completing the integration of what he knew in his mind with what he had experienced in his heart.

During his time in Arabia, Paul's leadership transformation became complete—he fully surrendered to God and God's plan for him, he began to trust in God's presence and provision, he became confident in God's unconditional love, and he accepted and abided in Jesus. He then returned to Damascus prepared to teach and equip.

One-on-One leadership

Once leaders have life in proper perspective through self-examination, they can develop a trusting relationship with others. Without trust, no organization can function effectively. Trust is essential for two people to work together. It is important to note, though, that the outcome of trust will never be achieved or maintained if the first arena of development, personal leadership, has not been addressed. If a leader has a self-serving perspective, people will never move toward him or her.

We can turn to Jesus again as our example of servant-hearted one-on-one leadership. At the beginning of His ministry, after spending time in the wilderness, where His life purpose and perspective were refined by trials and temptations, Jesus began the process of calling His disciples. Once they agreed to follow Him, Jesus spent three years building a culture of trust with those men. This trust between Jesus and His disciples would not have developed if Jesus had not first spent time in the wilderness deciding whom He would follow in life and whom He was going to be!

In life role relationships, trust is the stream on which vulnerability, caring, commitment, and grace flow between parents and children, husbands and wives, brothers and sisters, friends, and fellow citizens. Trust pours first from loving hearts committed to serving and supporting one another, through promises kept, encouragement and appreciation expressed, support and acceptance, repentance and apologies accepted, to reconciliation and restoration. Yet trust is a stream with a fragile environmental balance: once it is polluted, it will take time and effort to restore.

The always-present power to restore intimacy and broken trust is love. Read the following words from the apostle Paul, and ponder anew the cleansing and healing properties of love:

> *If I speak in the tongues of men or of angels, but do not have love, I am only a resounding gong or a clanging cymbal. 2 If I have the gift of prophecy and can fathom all mysteries and all knowledge, and if I have a faith that can move mountains, but do not have love, I am nothing. 3 If I give all I possess to the poor and give over my body to hardship that I may boast, but do not have love, I gain nothing. 4 Love is patient, love is kind. It does not envy, it does not boast, it is not proud. 5 It does not dishonor others, it is not self-seeking, it is not easily angered, it keeps no record of wrongs. 6 Love does not delight in evil but rejoices with the truth. 7 It always protects, always trusts, always hopes, always perseveres. 1 Corinthians 13:1-7 NIV*

In Conclusion

All leaders have strengths and weaknesses, none are perfect in the tasks or jobs that they handle. Therefore, it is so important for us to follow the One that never fails, "Jesus." Think of a time when you lost trust in a leader. How did you feel, what did you do? Knowing Jesus and how He "walked the walk and talked the talk" is vital to every person. Some people may not want to be a leader or serve in a leadership position, however, living life is a leadership position. You at a minimum must lead yourself in right and wrong decisions. Knowing the Word of God and following it as Jesus did will be an all-around help in everything we do with the calling on our lives.

True leadership comes from the heart, yes, a lot can be gotten from books and or classroom teachings, but without heart, leadership is dead works with a title and position. Resurrect the leader in yourself and others with the Word of God. Remember Jesus followed God and we need to follow Jesus as the perfect example in the same manner.

Leaders need training, and the quality of training they get will reflect their leadership level and ability. We all need refresher training as well as two-way conservational feedback from the people around us. God tells us in 2 Timothy 2,

Study to shew thyself approved unto

God, a workman that needeth not to be ashamed, rightly dividing the word of truth. 2 Timothy 2:15 KJV

This is not a one-time training; the study is ongoing refreshing and renewed training.

Someone that follows the leadership of Jesus is a leader of and for the people. The other is a destroyer also known as a dictator, who destroys the livelihood of people.

So, I encourage you, do not be the leader who lives only for the benefit of yourself, be a leader that will make lasting changes in the lives of others, and follow the leadership and love of Jesus.

Made in the USA
Columbia, SC
16 September 2024